Devotionals

by June Gordon

PRESENTED TO

_____

_____

_____

FROM

_____

_____

_____

Bite-sized meditations
from the minds and mouths
of grandchildren

This edition is published by special arrangement with and permission of Star Books, Inc., Wilson, NC. First edition © 1988.

All scripture quotations are taken from the New American Standard Bible © The Lockman Foundation, unless otherwise identified.

Much of the materials were originally published as *Grandma's Book* © 1988 by June Gordon and Star Books, Inc., and used by permission. All rights reserved.

This completely revised edition © 1990 by Meridian Publishing, Grand Rapids, MI. All rights reserved.

M10   ISBN 0-529-06852-4

Book and cover design by Gayle Raymer

Published with World Bible Publishers
Printed in the United States of America

*To my grandchildren
Kristin
and
Kara*

Let Them Come
For of Such Is the Kingdom

Precious, precious little ones
Down from heaven above;
By God's own miracle they come,
His gifts to us of love.

And in the depths of their blue eyes,
I am sure that I can see—
Way beyond the azure skies
A glimpse of God's eternity.

Contents

"Hewwo, Gwampa!"	9
No Santa Claus	11
God's Treasures	13
What a Mighty God We Serve	15
Shelter in the Storm	17
The Only Real Superman	19
"I Pinely Dot It Up"	21
The Mess	23
The Box of Matches	25
Behind the Tree	27
"Gwanma, Watch Me!"	29
Words Versus Actions	31
"Evweybody's Tumin"	33
The Recipe	34
"Candy's Such a Pain"	36
Loaded Pickups and Wrinkled Hands	37
Hot Jeans	39
"Not a Dress!"	41
Two Kinds of Faith	43
Where's the Sun?	44
Food for Thought	46
Fear Not	47
Private Clubhouse	49
"Write Me a Letter"	51
The Word	53
Faith or Presumption	55

The Junk Drawer	57
The Cleaning Service	59
"It's Mine!"	61
"My Smile Wouldn't Smile!"	63
Sharing the French Fries	65
"Just in Case"	67
Your Name	69
Good News and Bad News	71
"I Sure Needed That"	73
The Race	75
No Time to Switch	77
"Lifetime Lifeguard"	79

"Hewwo, Gwampa!"

Unless you are converted and become like children, you shall not enter the kingdom of heaven.
Matt. 18:3

Kristin was two, and Grandpa was just about her favorite person. She was Grandpa's favorite person, too.

Kristin had recently attained enough clarity of speech to talk on the phone, long distance, to Grandma and Grandpa. The extent of her conversation with me was usually, "Hewwo, Gwanma, wanna tawk to Gwampa."

But one day I had to tell her that her dearly beloved Grandpa had gone to Heaven. I told her that he wouldn't be sick anymore, and that he wouldn't have to have any more heart surgery.

She didn't want Grandpa to be sick, so it was all right. But she missed him, and pretty soon she thought it was time for him to come back.

One day her mother found her talking on the phone. "Kristin," she said, "you have your toy phone. You mustn't play with the real phone."

But Kristin replied firmly, "Gotta use the weal phone, Mommie. I'm callin' Hebbin. Jesus is gettin' Gwampa for me."

Mother walked from the room with tear-filled eyes, and let Kristin play with the "weal" phone.

Dear God, thank you that even a small child can find comfort in the knowledge of the great hereafter.

No Santa Claus

*You shall know the truth,
and the truth shall make you free.*
John 8:32

When Kristin was five, and Christmas was approaching, she was questioning her mother about Santa Claus. One of her questions was: "Does he take those clothes off when he goes to bed at night?"

Her mother realized that she was probing deeper than the clothes question and decided that perhaps the moment for truth had come. She had vowed never to lie to her children.

So now, Mother told Kristin that we give gifts to our loved ones in remembrance of that first Christmas, when God gave us his Son, the tiny baby Jesus. She tried to explain (hoping it wouldn't take the fun out of the holiday season) that Santa Claus is only a symbol of our love for each other at Christmas. Then she asked Kristin not to tell the other "kids", especially her little sister Kara, for it is fun to "pretend" when you are little.

Mother saw that Kristin was very quiet at this disclosure, but she didn't seem too upset.

When daddy came home for lunch, Kristin cupped her hand over the side of her mouth and hissed in a loud stage whisper, "Mommie, can we tell Daddy there's no Santa Claus?"

Dear heavenly Father, thank you for the Truth that you have given us, which sets us free from all the myths and fables so many believe in.

God's Treasures

*Eye has not seen and ear has not heard...
all that God has prepared
for those who love him.*
1 Cor. 2:9

I always take much pleasure in the weeks before Christmas in choosing small (and sometimes not so small) gifts for my two little granddaughters. They have been such a joy and comfort to me since I lost my husband.

First there was only Kristin, who was two when her Grandpa died; then, two years later, Kara was born.

I was always so thankful that my daughter and her husband were kind enough to bring the children to me on Christmas Eve, since our homes were quite a distance apart.

But one Christmas the three-hundred-mile trip was growing long and tiresome for two-year-old Kara, and she was fussing. Kristin, now six, comforted her little sister. "Kara, just wait until we get to Grandma's house. We will have hundreds of presents!"

Dear heavenly Father, when the way grows long and we feel weary, help us to remember there are treasures at the end.

What a Mighty God We Serve

*Before they call, I will answer;
and while they are still speaking, I will hear.*
Isa. 65:24

"It's me, Gwanma," the small voice on the phone replied in a vexed tone when I had asked, "Is this Kristin or Kara?" (My two-year-old granddaughter Kara's greeting had begun sometimes to sound like her older sister's voice.)

"Well, of course, honey, it's you," I soothed quickly. "And you're Kara, but you sounded so big!" She giggled, and I asked to speak to her mother.

After hanging up, I thought how often each day I call our heavenly Father and I don't even have to say, "It's me, God," for he knows who it is that calls.

What a mighty God we serve! He has so many children and still knows each of us personally—our voices, our thoughts, our needs, our aspirations, everything. It is too marvelous for me to grasp!

Dear heavenly Father, thank you that you are always on the line when I need you. And thank you that you know who I am!

Shelter in the Storm

*Lead me to the rock that is higher than I.
For you have been a refuge for me.*
Psa. 61:2,3

Daylight was breaking on a clear sky, though it had been a dark and stormy night with wind, thunder, lightning, and torrents of rain.

Kristin had become frightened and had taken her sleeping bag into her parents' bedroom. There she could sleep peacefully, knowing she would be cared for.

Later, Kara, too, had gone to her parents' bedroom to say scornfully to Kristin, "I not tared! I tay in my own bed."

I smile at Kara's superiority, for it is nice that she feels better than her sister in at least one way. Sometimes it is hard to be the little one in the family. But she is not always so brave. There are other things which frighten her, and she, too, runs just as quickly to Mother and Dad for shelter.

I remember the storms of life when I have sought safety and shelter. When my husband died, the only way I could sleep at night was to repeat, "In peace I will both lie down and sleep, for you alone, O Lord, make me to dwell in safety" (Psa. 4:8).

I was, for sure, placing my sleeping bag close to my heavenly Parent.

Dear heavenly Father, thank you for shelter and safety during the storms of life!

The Only Real Superman

*He is the one who took God's wrath
against our sins upon himself,
and brought us into fellowship with God;
and he is the forgiveness for our sins,
and not only ours, but all the world's.*
1 John 2:2 TLB

Two-year-old Kara swooped up beside my chair, arms flying, and announced, "I'm Superman!"

"That's nice," I replied. "Are you rescuing someone?"

She nodded solemnly. I asked, "How about giving Grandma a kiss?"

She squared her small shoulders, put her hands on her hips, and with blue eyes flashing replied sternly, "No, tourse not! Superman nevah divs tisses!" Arms flailing, she ran off to her next imaginary rescue.

I smiled at her play as I meditated on the only true Superman our race has ever known—our Lord Jesus Christ, who died to rescue us all.

And he gives love with his rescues!

Dear heavenly Father, thank you for loving us so much that you sent your Son to give us eternal life. And thank you that your Son loved us enough to die for us.

"I Pinely Dot It Up"

*Your ears will hear a word behind you,
"This is the way, walk in it,"
whenever you turn to the right or to the left.*
Isa. 30:21

The late June sunshine was pleasant, one of those marvelous spring days when you are glad for life, whatever troublesome thoughts might try to depress you.

I was weeding my garden with hoe and trowel. Little Kara was with me. She had an old spoon and was also digging here and there.

Cares were pressing and I wasn't paying much attention to her, until I heard her exclamation of delight.

"I pinely dot it up!" She ran to show me. "See, Gwanma. I pinely dot it up!" She had. Roots and all. It was a tomato plant.

She could tell by my face that I was not too pleased with her good job. Her small face fell. She had only wanted to help.

And I wondered, do I sometimes go to the Lord to show him what I have finally accomplished—with great effort— and find he didn't want me to do it at all?

Dear Lord, please help me to clear my mind of my own desires, and to listen more quietly for your directions.

The Mess

*What's the use of saying
that you have faith and are Christians
if you aren't proving it by helping others?*
James 2:14 TLB

There is a meticulous housekeeping streak in my husband's family which has surfaced in my youngest granddaughter, Kara. At two, she sometimes folds her dirty clothes!

One day, she walked into the family room of the home from which I was moving and exclaimed, "Gwanma, dis house is a mess!"

"Yes, honey," I explained, "but Grandma is moving. I have to mess things up because I'm going to a new home."

But Kara wasn't listening. She walked into the next room and exclaimed with even more disgust, "Dis is a wuss mess!"

Kristen, her older sister, didn't mind the mess. She cast a practiced eye around for anything that might look like it was worth salvaging.

I thought, *Sometimes the world looks like such a mess to us, God. You have tried to explain what you are doing, but we haven't listened very well.*

Dear Lord, when we see the troubles around us, please help us not to criticize. Please help us to do as Kristin did, to cast our eyes around for anything that we might salvage for your kingdom.

The Box of Matches

The earth is the Lord's, and all it contains.
1 Cor. 10:26

Kristin had come with her dad when he was helping me with moving. I was cleaning out a kitchen drawer and had put two boxes of matches on the table.

"Grandma, can I have these?" Kristin asked. I looked questioningly at her dad. Matches weren't usually something a child might want or need. Kristen continued, "We need them to light our fireplace."

Her dad didn't say no, so I replied, "Well, yes, Kristen, I guess you can have one of the boxes. But be sure to give it to Mother as soon as you get home."

"Thank you, Grandma," she said. I noticed that one box was nearly empty and the other was full. She took the full one. Then, hesitating a moment, she opened it and placed a generous handful of matches in my nearly empty one.

"There, Grandma," she said. "I gave you some so you don't run out."

I wasn't too impressed, since all the

matches had been mine in the beginning. But it was apparent that she felt some sort of commendation was in order. So I said gravely, "Thank you, Kristin. That was nice of you," and she grinned happily.

I realized suddenly that sometimes I treat the Lord in a like manner. I come to him and say, "Look, God, I gave you more than your tithe!" And I forget it was all his in the beginning!

Gracious heavenly Father, thank you for all your gifts. Help us not to rob you in tithes and offerings when you have been so generous with us.

Behind the Tree

*Everyone who shall confess me before men,
I will also confess him before my Father
who is in heaven.*
Matt. 10:32

It was Kristin's first day of school. I remembered such a day, long past in my motherhood, and sympathized with my daughter as she related the pangs of the day.

Tears glistened in her eyes as she told me, "And there I was to meet the bus. I wanted to see how my little darling was and she didn't even want to see me!" Then she laughed. "I guess I should have hidden behind a tree. When I tried to take her hand she said, 'Don't take my hand, Mommie. I'm a big girl now, you know!' Then she looked warily at the departing bus to see if anyone had noticed Mother had come to meet her."

I reassured my daughter that I was certain Kristin was glad to see her, even though she didn't acknowledge it.

Do you suppose we sometimes treat our heavenly Father as Kristin did her mother? Do we sometimes fail to acknowledge him as our heavenly Parent, or let the world see we are Christians who depend on him? Do we try to hide our faith behind a tree? And could it be that there are tears in God's eyes as he watches over us and longs for us to come closer?

Dear God, please help us never to be too proud to acknowledge that you are our Strength and Source.

"Gwanma, Watch Me!"

*Since we have so great a
cloud of witnesses surrounding us...
let us run with endurance the
race that is set before us.*
Heb. 12:1

No one passing through Moundville, Missouri (population 194) on Highway 43 would ever guess that at one time it had been a thriving mining town, with stores, a bank, and even a college! Now, the old brick buildings and streets are mostly deserted with one exception.

Once a year Moundville has a homecoming picnic and its former citizens flock back. The local villagers and farmers extend their hands in welcome and do their very best to entertain the visitors. They begin with a parade in the morning which far surpasses most local parades.

Participating in this parade was a highlight of my children's growing-up years. Though Kristin and Kara live too far away to have their own entry in the parade, generous relatives have always made a place on a float for them. And they love participating.

Last summer in order for me to attend the homecoming celebration, I had to work overtime and drive a long way. As the miles sped by, I wondered wearily if it was worth it.

But, after the parade Kara hugged me happily and chortled, "I taw you! I taw you! Gwanma watched me!" I knew then it had been worth all my efforts to get there. I had no idea it would mean so much to her to see Grandma's face among the bystanders.

Paul said we all have a great cloud of onlookers in heaven. I have often wondered how our loved ones in heaven can be happy if they see us struggling here. And am I as happy for my loved ones to be watching me as Kara was for Grandma to be watching her? Not always, I'm afraid.

Dear Lord, if the verse truly means what it seems to; if our loved ones are watching our progress; please help me to walk a little closer to you.

Words Versus Actions

*You were formerly darkness,
but now you are light in the Lord;
walk as children of light.*
Eph. 5:8

Kristin's first week of school was over, and we all wanted to know if she had really liked it. We wanted her first-grade days to be happy, because first grade is such an important foundation for school. And school is a crucial part of our growing-up years.

Kristin sensing our concern, reported dutifully that she *really* liked school. I thought she seemed a little too quiet, however. I wasn't surprised when she confided to her Aunt Janice that she really liked it, but didn't want to go back.

As a child, I sang a chorus, "Isn't It Grand to Be a Christian?" And it is grand to be a Christian. I could never survive without my faith. And we try to tell the world that we really like being Christians. But sometimes we don't act very joyful or happy in our Christian walk!

Dear heavenly Father, please help our actions to be true expressions of your love and the joy of serving you. Please help us, Lord, by your grace to be the light of the world, that others might be drawn into your kingdom.

"Evweybody's Tumin"

*Go out into the highways and along
the hedges, and compel them to come in,
that my house may be filled.*
Luke 14:23

Little Kara was ecstatic, running to meet me as I got out of the car.

"Gwanma!" she shouted gleefully. "I'm having a burfday party and evweybody's tumin!"

And they were. All the ones she wanted to invite, the aunts, uncles, and cousins who loved the little miss just turning three. I am sure it was a day she will never forget.

And I am reminded of another banquet in a story Jesus told. The invited guests didn't come to this banquet, so the master of the house went out into the highways and byways to find people to celebrate the feast he had prepared.

I am sorry, Lord, for the people who were invited and didn't come. But I am glad that your Servant found me, out on the lonely highway, and carried me in.

Thank you, thank you, thank you for including me in your family.

The Recipe

*Therefore, however you want people
to treat you, so treat them.
Matt. 7:12*

Kara's daddy was planning to make homemade ice cream for her third birthday party, and he asked me if I had a good recipe. I told him I was sorry, but I didn't have one. Homemade ice cream had never been one of my specialties.

Six-year-old Kristin spread her hands and advised in a superior tone, "Why it's easy. All you need is ice and the ingredients! (She seems to have learned many things since starting school.)

I laughed as I told her, "That's not exactly true, Kristin. You need one more thing—the recipe."

I think of how our Lord has given us a life and all the ingredients for happiness. He has even given us the recipe. Yet most of us are miserable some of the time, and some of us are miserable most of the time.

Dear Lord, it isn't that your recipe doesn't work. I am afraid we haven't used it. Please help us to do better.

"Candy's Such a Pain!"

*I am with you always,
even to the end of the age.*
Matt. 28:20

I was surprised when Kristin joined me as I worked in the yard. I thought she had gone with Aunt Janice to take our little dog Candy for a walk. When I asked why she hadn't gone too, she replied, "Just Kara went. That Candy's such a pain. I decided to stay home!"

What she said about Candy is quite true. Having run at large most of her life, Candy does not take too kindly to city life and walking on a leash. In all honesty, taking her for a walk is such a major undertaking that I seldom try.

I find myself wondering suddenly in my heart if my walk with Jesus might sometimes be a "pain" for him. Like Candy, do I take a path so wayward, so erratic and undisciplined that Jesus is just tempted to stay home? I hope not.

Dear Lord, please don't grow weary of guiding my footsteps, even though they are often stubborn and willful.

Loaded Pickups and Wrinkled Hands

Man looks at the outward appearance, but the Lord looks at the heart.
1 Sam. 16:7

"But why, Kristin? Why don't you want to ride with Grandma?" I couldn't believe she would pass up the chance for a ride to the store with Kara and Grandma to get a small treat.

Kristin flushed, but held her ground. "It's 'cause you got stuff in the back of your pickup!"

"But, Kristin!" I sputtered. "That's what pickups are for!"

Her mother laughed and said, "Oh, don't mind her, Mom. She won't ride with her dad either, when he has something in his pickup."

I thought how foolish it was for a mere child to be so concerned about appearances.

But as Kara and I went for the treat she requested, I noticed my hands on the steering wheel. And I thought remorsefully that perhaps I am as foolish as Kristin.

So often of late I have been ashamed of my hands. I work with a lovely younger woman, whose smooth, unlined hands fly over the keys of the computer and adding machine. My own hands are wrinkled; they look old; and they move a little more slowly on the machines.

But just as my little pickup was made to haul things, my hands were made to work. My hands have changed diapers and tended gardens. They have cooked, canned, and scrubbed floors. They have soothed a sick child's feverish brow. And in-between times, they have typed, taken shorthand, run an adding machine, and now a computer. These hands have been folded in prayer through long night watches of illness and death.

Dear heavenly Father, it is hard to grow old in a world that values youth and beauty. Thank you, God, for my hands. You gave them to me to use. Help me to remember that it is not the outward appearance that matters as much as the beauty of the heart. Please help me, Lord, to have a kind and loving heart.

Hot Jeans

*The Lord knows full well
how the human mind reasons,
and how foolish and futile it is.*
1 Cor. 3:20 TLB

Three-year-old Kara was in tears. As I came up the walk, I saw that her small, expressive face was devastated by some great sorrow. I ran to her and asked with concern, "Honey, what is the matter?"

Tears were streaming from the blue eyes. "Mama won't let me wear jeans," she sobbed. It was a very warm, late summer evening.

"But, sweetie," I said, "it's too hot for jeans!" Tears continued to flow. Her mother came to the door.

"It's hopeless, Mom. She has only wanted to wear jeans all summer. She knows they are hot. She says, 'Can I wear my *hot* jeans?'"

Mother was right, but reasoning didn't help. Before the evening was over, Kara, had jeans on.

The next time I visited, fall had descended, and the night was damp and chilly. I was surprised when I came in to see that Kara had shorts on.

"Honey, where are your jeans?" I asked. "You will catch cold!" She merely gave me a big smile, a hug, and a kiss before continuing her play.

Her mother said again, "It's hopeless, Mom. She wears hot jeans in the summer. In the winter, it looks like she is going to wear shorts. I give up." I didn't say anything.

I am learning. Slowly! And I am wondering. Are my prayers to the heavenly Father sometimes so out of order that he feels like giving up on me? There is a hymn that begins: "Dear Lord and Father of mankind, forgive our foolish ways." I think my little granddaughter's actions are a portrayal of man's "foolish ways."

Dear Lord, if my petitions are sometimes foolish as hot jeans in the summer and shorts in the winter, please be patient with me, for I am made of dust.

"Not a Dress!"

*If you then, being evil,
know how to give good gifts to your children,
how much more shall your Father
who is in heaven give
what is good to those who ask him!*
Matt. 7:11

Kristin's seventh birthday was approaching and her mother had asked me to give her a new dress to wear to church. I was aware that such a present might not be Kristin's choice, but I knew she needed a dress. As it came time for my athletic little one to open her pretty package, she exclaimed, "I sure hope it's not a dress!"

And, of course, it was. But she decided she liked it anyhow, especially when Sunday came and she had something new and pretty to wear.

I found myself recalling times I had petitioned Father God for help, and I didn't always appreciate the answers that came, only to realize later that they were for the best!

Dear heavenly Father, forgive me when I don't appreciate your gifts. Please help me to know they are always good gifts—even though I may not realize it at the time.

Two Kinds of Faith

*I say to you, not even in Israel
have I found such great faith.*
Luke 7:9

I was attempting to make Kristin and Kara some cool summer dresses. I really am not a very proficient seamstress, and I suggested to the girls that they should pray for me so that I might complete their dresses on the limited time schedule I had.

The next morning as I tried the dresses on the girls, I said again that they should pray for Jesus to help Grandma.

"I already did! Twelve times!" Kristin replied. "But I will again."

Then Kara said slowly and thoughtfully, "I prayed last night! But I'll 'mind God."

I told their mother my faith was more like Kristin's than Kara's. I make my requests to God a dozen times at least, if not more.

Incidentally, Kara's dress was finished first.

*D*ear heavenly Father, I'm remembering my early childhood years when my faith was fresh and untarnished by doubts. Please help me to have such faith again!

Where's the Sun?

*And God made the two great lights,
the greater light to govern the day,
and the lesser light to govern the night.*
Gen. 1:16

For some time I had been looking forward to the extra hour of sleep that accompanies going off daylight-saving time. Each morning, it had been harder and harder to shake off the night's slumber. And that weekend I stayed with Kristin and Kara while their mother and daddy were out of town.

In the dark of the much anticipated night, I felt a little presence beside my bed. Kara. She whispered, "Gwanma! Gwanma! It's time for the sun to tum up!"

I squinted at the clock. Four o'clock and since I hadn't turned the clock back yet, that was daylight savings time. Even in my befuddled, sleepy state of mind I figured that by real time it was only three.

I pulled her into bed with me, rubbing her cold feet as I said, "No, sweetie pie, the sun won't be up for a long time yet! We have lots of time to sleep!"

But she didn't believe me. She insisted,

"No, Gwanma, I know it's time for the sun to tum up!" For over three hours we discussed the matter, with her dozing restlessly for a few minutes between inquiries of "Where is dat sun?"

Finally, I gave up. I was not rested, but I was definitely awake! Downstairs I began, with much help, to make a pie for Sunday dinner and muffins for breakfast. At last the sun did appear, peeking through the east window. Kara was overjoyed.

"Dere it is, Gwanma—dere it is! The sun did tum up!"

How wonderful that after each night there is a morning! How much we take for granted in our world. We never doubt the natural sequence of events which a loving heavenly Father has ordered.

Dear Lord, thank you for the day and for the night. Thank you for seedtime and harvest and for all the things you have so lovingly provided for us, which we seldom think about.

Food for Thought

*It is written,
Man shall not live on bread alone.*
Luke 4:4

I was fixing myself a sandwich before starting my trip home. Kara was dogging my steps. I asked her if she would like to eat a sandwich with Grandma. She hesitated a minute, then stated firmly, "No, Gwanma, I need some *weal* food."

And so do I, I thought, remembering how neglectful I have been of the real food needed in my Christian life. For lately I haven't found, or taken, the time to read and study my Bible as I should. No wonder I feel down. I haven't fed my spiritual body!

Dear heavenly Father, forgive me when I don't give my spiritual body the food it needs to survive. Help me to remember that even your Son, Jesus, had need of the written word.

Fear Not

*You will not be afraid of the terror by night,
or of the arrow that flies by day.*
Psa. 91:5

I was looking after Kristin and Kara. Kristin was playing with some neighbor children across the street; and Kara, just up from her nap, wanted one of two things: for Grandma to come outside and play with her, or to go across the street to play with the other children. However, she was afraid to cross the street alone.

I told her I was too busy right now to play with her, but that she could call Kristin to come help her across the street.

Soon Kara was back by my side, fighting tears. "Gwanma, Kwistin won't wistin to me!"

I washed and dried my hands, for I had been preparing vegetables. I took Kara's hand and went outside. When I called for Kristin to come get Kara, she heard, and started to come at once. But before she could take more than two steps across the street, Kara, with a squeal of joy, and not looking either way, dashed across the street to her trusted older sister.

I marveled at Kara's complete lack of fear when her sister was close.

"Do I trust my Savior that much?" I asked myself.

Dear Lord, when the way ahead looks frightening, help me to know it's safe if you are there.

Private Clubhouse

Has Christ been divided?
1 Cor. 1:13

When we had some remodeling done, I had the contractor build Kristin and Kara a tree house in our huge elm.

One day I told Kara how a little neighbor girl enjoyed playing in their tree house when they weren't there. I thought it would interest Kara to know that other children thought their tree house was nice. But her big blue eyes clouded a little, and she said, "Gwanma, when you get home, I want you to put a sign on our tree house! I want you to put a big sign that says, 'Pwivate Clubhouse.'"

"Oh, really?" I asked.

"Yes," she said firmly, and added, "Put Pwivate Clubhouse—Kwistin, Kara, Gwanma and Aunt Janice *only*!"

I tried to demonstrate that things are more enjoyable when shared, but I don't think I was successful in convincing her. She still wanted the sign on the tree house!

Occasionally, I have attended churches where I felt there should have been a sign at the door that said, "Private Club."

We are all sure that our own church, with its particular doctrine, is the best, and sometimes it is hard to accept others if their beliefs differ. I wonder if the only true way we can be "best" is in accepting with love all people who believe in Christ as their Savior, and have been baptized in his precious name. For Christ is not divided.

Dear heavenly Father, we are all branches of one Tree. Please help us not to create division.

"Write Me a Letter"

*My little children,
I am writing these things to you...*
1 John 2:1

When the phone rang, a small voice demanded, "Gwanma, I want you to write me a letter."

"Oh?" I said, wondering what had brought on this abrupt request.

"And," the wee voice continued, "Do it wight now! Like you used to Kwistin."

And then my questioning mind knew. Kristin had told Kara how I had written her story/letters when she started preschool. My motive had been to kindle in my little outdoors girl some interest in the necessary skills of reading and writing. In the stories I had emphasized one key letter, which I used repeatedly, and promised Kristin a dollar when she sent me a paper on which she had practiced writing this letter several times.

So now I said to the demanding little voice on the phone reassuringly, "Okay, Kara, Grandma will send you a letter. Just as soon as I have time. I promise."

I have a friend, who, during a perplexing period of her life, said she wished God would drop a letter in her mailbox. Actually, God did write us a letter, a long time ago, and there are key words in it—words like "love" and "forgiveness", that he wants us to practice.

Dear God, please help me to read your letter. For if I try, I can find the answers there to all my problems.

The Word

In the beginning was the Word...
John 1:1

I had at last found time to write Kara the requested story/letters. And, as I had with Kristin, I offered to give her a dollar for the sheets she returned to me on which she had practiced writing certain letters.

To get as much mileage out of my efforts as possible, I also told first-grader Kristin (still my little outdoors girl who would rather run than read or write) that I would give her a dime per word for the words she could think of that began with that same letter. But I soon found this offer rather foolhardy! I had in mind around ten words. She never had less than twenty!

Then one Sunday, my granddaughters came with their mother and daddy for dinner, bringing the latest completed sheets. I was aghast at the number of words Kristin had on her sheet. I puzzled over the list of neatly written words. Where had she come up with all of them? Her mother said she hadn't helped her.

At last, the answer came. Aunt Janice told me that Kristin had used the dictionary.

When I mentally picked myself up off the floor (after imagining paying ten cents for every word in the dictionary) I tried to plan a course of action to get Grandma out of the corner she had worked herself into.

When I found Kristin alone, I told her how proud I was of her for thinking of using the dictionary. She beamed until I went on to explain that Grandma wanted her not only to write the words, but also to know their meaning.

As I tried to explain to her that a word is useless to us, unless we know the meaning, I suddenly found conviction in my own heart. For I have often read God's word, without thinking and meditating on the depth of the message it contains.

Dear Lord, please help us not only to read your word, but to pray for understanding too.

Faith or Presumption

*If you have faith as a mustard seed,
you shall say to this mountain,
'Move from here to there,' and it shall move;
and nothing shall be impossible to you.*
Matt. 17:20

In trying to strengthen my faith, I have read books and articles by those who advocate that when you ask God for something, you should immediately begin thanking him for the answered prayer. I have always had a little trouble with this theory—in spite of the scripture which tells us that according to our faith, so it will be to us. I have always wondered. *Isn't that a bit presumptuous? Presuming on God's mercy?*

An example of such faith might have been innocently portrayed one morning by my little Kara. She is always an early riser, but especially on Saturday, when she knows everyone is going to be at home. Why waste a minute of such an interesting day?

One Saturday Kara was attempting, without much success, to get her mama and daddy up. She had joined them in their bed, but all of her rolling, tumbling, and pleading had not done much good. At last she closed her eyes, folded her hands, and said, "Thank you, Jesus, for this food. Amen." Then she promptly opened her eyes and announced, "There, Mommie. I've 'turned thanks. Now get me my breakfast!"

Faith or presumption? I don't know. But her mother got up and got her breakfast. Maybe I'd better read those books again!

Dear Lord, I do believe. Help my unbelief.

The Junk Drawer

*First take the log out of your own eye,
and then you will see clearly to take the speck
out of your brother's eye.*
Matt. 7:5

Does everyone have a junk drawer in their kitchen? We do, I'm afraid. There are pliers and a small hammer, if you dig long enough to find them. There are ties for garbage bags, twine, miscellaneous screws and nails, and among other things, the remnants of last year's garden seeds. In all honesty, it is a mess!

On one of her visits, I directed Kristin to the junk drawer when she wanted some twine for one of her enterprises. She viewed the disarray, then remarked, "Mama has a junk drawer too—but she cleans it out once in a while!" I smiled at the innocent candor of her remark, and the clear implication that ours hadn't been cleaned out for a while. She was right, it hadn't.

And I think of how the other person's faults, the junk drawers of their lives, always look worse to us than our own. Surely their bad habits are worse than ours!

Dear Lord, please help me to be charitable in my thoughts of others. Please help me to remember that with the judgment I have for others, I will be measured by the same standard. So, please, God, help me to look first at my own faults.

The Cleaning Service

*Neither did we eat anyone's bread...
but we kept working day and night.*
2 Thess. 3:8

On my granddaughters' visits, I never know what Kristin's busy little mind is going to come up with next. She is now eight, and whatever venture she embarks upon, four-year-old Kara is usually just about two steps behind.

One day when they came into the kitchen where I was working, Kristin was carrying a box of various and assorted articles, which she set down importantly. Then she announced, "We're in the cleaning business! We've come to help you clean."

"Well, how nice," I murmured, "Grandma could use some help." Then I proceeded to give out my assignments. "Kristin, you can make your beds; and Kara, you can dust in the living room."

Kristin considered this proposal for about one minute, as she shifted from one foot to the other. Then she explained, "Oh, no. We don't do the work. We just give advice."

I sighed. I had been sure there was a catch someplace.

So many people would like to be in an advisory position and forget about the hard labor. I remembered Paul, the faithful apostle in the Bible, who worked steadfastly as he preached, thereby setting an example in deed as well as words.

Dear heavenly Father, please let my life be a life of good deeds, as well as good words.

"It's Mine!"

*Even if a man is caught in any trespass...
restore such a one in a spirit of gentleness.*
Gal. 6:1

Kara, at four, became very much absorbed in listening to tapes and enjoying music. She used her mother and daddy's tape recorder constantly. They decided, therefore, to give her a tape recorder of her own for Christmas.

She was, quite naturally, very proud of her new possession. At the family Christmas dinner, she was walking around, holding it on top of her head. Her Great-aunt Glenna cautioned, "You might drop that!"

"It's mine!" Kara replied with a cool look.

I am reminded of the times when our actions are not in accordance with our Father's teachings, but if we feel a gentle nudge of reproof from a minister or friend, we say, "Well, it's my life!"

Then when we crash, we plead, "Oh, God, help us!" And many times the help comes through God's servants whose advice we have previously disdained.

Dear God, help me to accept, with grace, a well-intentioned criticism offered with love from a friend. For King Solomon said, "He who hates reproof is a fool."

"My Smile Wouldn't Smile!"

*For the good that I wish, I do not do;
but I practice the very evil that I do not wish.*
Rom. 7:19

Ours has always been a singing family. So, since the day after the family Christmas reunion was Sunday, all the cousins were enjoying being together and presenting a song service in the small local church where our clan had its roots.

There were now several third generation little ones running around, and since many of them showed the potential of becoming good singers, it was decided to let them join in the singing.

This was Kristin's first experience in singing a solo at church, and she did very well. However, I could tell she was frightened. Afterward she said, "Grandma, my smile wouldn't smile!"

How often in my life I have wanted to do the things I should, to smile and be of encouragement to others, but I couldn't seem to do it. I am thankful for the faithful apostle in the Bible who admitted he had the same experience. Knowing that such a great saint had the same problem as I, gives me the courage to keep on trying!

Dear Lord, I have failed so many times in the things I felt you wanted me to do. Please, by your love and grace, help me to do better.

Sharing the French Fries

*For I was hungry, and
you gave me something to eat...
to the extent that you did it to one of
these brothers, you did it to me.*
Matt. 24:35,40

We had promised Kristin and Kara lunch at McDonald's after the song service at church. So although there were other places I might have preferred to eat on Sunday, we took them to McDonald's.

Kristin and Kara ordered their usual "Happy Meals." I didn't order any french fries with my sandwich, since the children never ate all those which came with their food.

I dumped a few from Kara's box on my tray before spreading her lunch before her. Then I noticed that Aunt Janice didn't have any fries, and I asked if she wanted some of the ones on my tray.

"Oh, I'm sharing Kristin's," she replied. Kristin, looking askance at the hand in her fries, said, "But don't take anymore! I might need them!"

We smile at her natural childish tendency for self-preservation and then I think of all the hungry people in the world. We are so well fed. We do want to help them, but first we want to be sure we will always have enough for ourselves!

Dear heavenly Father, I am not a child. Please help me to be more faithful in my efforts to help the unfortunate. For you have said they are your children too.

"Just in Case"

*A friend loves at all time,
and a brother is born for adversity.*
Prov. 17:17

No Christmas is complete until Kristin and Kara have stayed a few days with Grandma and Aunt Janice. On this visit we were sitting on the divan, looking at old pictures of their mama and Aunt Janice, when they were little girls.

Suddenly I noticed Kara's face was slightly pale. Since she had been very ill during the night, I asked anxiously, "Kara, honey, do you feel all right?"

Kara looked dubious, as if she wasn't really sure, but she said she was all right. Kristin, who had been sitting beside her, looked startled for a moment; then she scrambled up and moved to the other side of Aunt Janice.

"Well, I'm going to sit over here—just in case!" she said.

We laugh at Kristin's practical self-protection, and I think how this same protectionist attitude often operates in friendships. As long as our friends' lives are in harmony, we love them. But if trouble arises, or if their reputations are damaged by faulty actions, we distance ourselves! Perhaps we don't want any of the "fall-out" to land on us.

And so it is, at the time when a person needs friendship the most, it is often not there!

Dear Lord, please let me always be a true friend whatever the circumstances.

Your Name

I know you by name.
Ex. 33:12

A small seedling oak had emerged in my yard. It grew with such vigor that I decided to transplant it to a more likely spot, one where it would have more room to grow into a mighty oak.

Kristin and Kara were visiting, and Kara, at four, was still interested in Grandma's outside activities. As she watched me carefully press dirt around the roots, she asked, "Gwanma, do you ever name your plants?"

"Well, no, Kara, I guess I never have," I replied. "Do you think we should?"

"Yes," she responded, "I think we should. Let's call this tree Gary!"

I told her that name would be fine with me. After that, each time she saw me watering outside, she would ask, "Have you watered Gary yet?"

I wonder that a little one is interested enough in a tree to name it and to care about its welfare. But I wonder more, in fact, I marvel, that our heavenly Father knows each one of us and cares about our welfare. Although we are such minute entities in his great universe, his all-enveloping love calls us each by name!

Dear heavenly Father, sometimes I feel so unimportant—so worthless. Then I remember that you know my name, and that you love me, and I know that I am of value. Please help me to impart the knowledge of your great love to others!

Good News and Bad News

*For God so loved the world,
that he gave his only begotten Son,
that whoever believes in him should not perish,
but have eternal life.*
John 3:16

Kristin was three when I took care of her for a week. Her mother was doing a long-term job as a substitute teacher, and Kristin had grown unhappy about going to a babysitter.

One day as I peeled potatoes for the evening meal, she came in from the backyard where she had been playing. She stood beside me and said, "Gwanma?"

"Yes, sweetie?"

She stood with legs firmly planted, her blue, blue eyes dead serious. She said, "I got tum good news, and tum bad news for you!"

As I considered this grown-up announcement from a three-year-old child, I wondered where she had heard it. Then I said, "I guess I'll take the good news first."

She said solemnly, "Well, the good news is, I want you to tum outside and pay wif me." She paused before adding a note of dire gloom: "and the bad news is, you don't haf to if you don't want to!"

So, needless to say, Grandma went outside and pushed Kristin's swing. I knew there would always be meals to prepare, but I would not always have a little granddaughter who wanted me to play with her. As I swung her, I thought of the Good News and the bad news that God has for the world. The Good News is that he sent us a Savior! The bad news is that we don't have to accept him if we don't want to.

Dear heavenly Father, thank you for the Good News the angels sang so long ago; "For unto you a Savior is born." Thank you that my mother told it to me when I was just a little child.

"I Sure Needed That"

*He went away grieved;
for he was one who owned much property.*
Matt. 19:22

The Easter Kristin was three, and before we had baby Kara, her family came home for a visit. Uncle Fred brought Kristin a huge, two-foot-tall, chocolate Easter bunny. I had never seen Kristin's blue eyes get so big, as she exclaimed softly. "I ture needed that!" Grandma wasn't really sure she needed it, but the big chocolate bunny made her very happy.

There are so many things in this world we think we need, to make us happy! Some we do need, and some would probably come under the category of "wanting." I do believe God wants us to have the good things he has placed in his creation.

He gave his servant Abraham many blessings. But our heavenly Father doesn't want us to place our other desires above loving him. He even tested his servant Abraham to be sure that he wasn't making an idol of the son that God had given him.

We have so many wonderful blessings to enjoy in this fleeting life, and we do grow so busy accumulating pleasant possessions.

Dear heavenly Father, help us not to become so involved in worldly things that we forget to give first place to our Creator and to accepting the Savior he sent us. For Jesus said, "What shall a man give in exchange for his soul?" (A soul which is going to live forever in eternity and only a few decades here on earth.)

Please, don't let me ever lose sight of my first need: faith in you and love for you, my Savior, because you first loved me.

The Race

*I have finished the course,
I have kept the faith.
2 Tim. 4:7*

Kristin's dad often ran in marathons, and it was her highest desire and ambition, that memorable summer when she was three, to run in a "wace" like her daddy. There was finally a contest for children under twelve. Well, she was way under, but Daddy decided to let her enter, and he would run with her.

He didn't think she would finish the course, which was half-a-mile long, but she surprised him. Though half-a-mile is a long way for little three-year-old legs, she kept going. Sometimes she had to sit down and rest, but after a little while, she always got up and trotted off again.

The officials were probably getting slightly weary of waiting for the last little contestant to come into view. Her daddy said that all the other entrants had gone home and the sun was setting, but sometimes my son-in-law exaggerates! However, Kristin didn't realize she was so far behind the others. As she wearily and happily crossed the finish line, she looked up at her father and asked, "Did I win, Daddy?"

There is a course in life we all must run. Sometimes we do grow weary, but when we rest a while, God gives us strength to go on. And we will all win, if we have accepted Christ as our Savior. Even if I am the last one in, there will be a crown of eternal life waiting for me!

Dear heavenly Father, when I finish my course and have kept the faith—the first glorious ten thousand years will have just begun. For this, I thank you.

No Time to Switch

*Be on the alert then,
for you do not know the day nor the hour
when the Son of man will come.*
Matt. 25:13

Janice and I were playing a card game with Kristin, eight, and Kara, four, one evening during a summer visit. Kara and I were partners, for at four, she was a little small to follow the rules. But she laid the cards down for me and was very excited whenever "we" won.

During one game, however, my little partner suddenly left me and switched over to Aunt Janice's lap. I soon saw why. Aunt Janice had only three cards left. Kara had decided that Aunt Janice was going to win and she wanted to be in partnership with the winner!

We laughed at Kara's lack of loyalty, and she laughed with us. Then it became part of the game for Kara to count everyone's remaining cards, and to try to switch partners in time to be with the winner.

On impulse, I asked the little ones, "But

whose side do you really want to be on, in this old world?" Kristin, whom Janice and I had been allowing to win most often, shouted, "Mine! Mine!"

But Kara knew Grandma had a deeper reason for her question, and she stated quickly, "We have to be on God's side!"

I felt moisture in my eyes at the steadfast faith of a little four-year-old and I told her, "You're right, Kara! Grandma is proud of you for thinking of that." Then I said a silent prayer that these two precious little girls would always be on God's side, for there will be a time for all of us when there is no "time to switch."

Thank you, dear God, that a seed of faith can take root in a little one's heart. Jesus told us that wise men hurry past and ignore your truths, but it has pleased you to reveal them to babes. I thank you, Lord, that no one is too small for your love.

"Lifetime Lifeguard"

*He will cover you with his pinions,
and under his wings you may seek refuge.*
Psa. 91:4

Aunt Janice had taken Kristin, eight, and Kara, four, swimming. When they came back home, they were excited and thrilled. Kara could touch the bottom and still keep her nose above water in the big pool. This year she could go with Kristin! No more "baby pool" for her! Of course, she had to be very careful, for she really wasn't an experienced swimmer. A step or two too far, and the water would be over her head.

"I help her," Kristin said proudly. "I watch her real close." Then she added happily, "I'm Kara's lifetime, lifeguard!"

I smiled at their enthusiasm and thought how nice it is to have a sister for a friend, a lifetime lifeguard.

And I thought, too, that actually we all have a lifetime Lifeguard when we choose to accept Christ as our Savior. For he has promised that he will be with us always—even to the end of the world. We don't have to fear when the storms of life rage, and the billows are high, for they won't go over our heads! In him, we have a lifetime Lifeguard who is always on duty.

Dear heavenly Father, thank you that Jesus taught us to pray: "Lead us not into temptation, but deliver us from evil." Thank you that we can place our trust in you and be safe.